Kreepy Katering

By Kaye Hamm

Hamm Publishing
6710 Finian Drive
Wilmington, North Carolina 28409

Photography by :

Kaye Hamm

All photographs and content are the property of Hamm Publishing. Do not duplicate without written consent.

Copyright 2006 by Kaye Hamm

Photographs copyright 2006 by Kaye Hamm

All rights reserved. No portion of this book may be reproduced without written permission.

ISBN 978-0-6151-6756-5

Dedication

To my long suffering family: my husband Todd, my children Patrick, Kelsey and Colin, who have endured endless days of my creepy obsession. I would like to thank my Halloween partner in crime Susan McConnell for all her help and input on this project. A special thanks to my daughter Kelsey for her creative input.

Forward

Every year I have a Halloween party for my closest friends and their families. I like my parties to be realistic not cute. I enjoy seeing people get grossed out by my props and mostly by my food. While searching for books with appropriate foods I found that there really were none for a party with truly realistic dishes. An idea was born.

I decided that I would fill the void for a creepy cookbook. These recipes are all very tasty regardless of appearance. I find that if you add food coloring and give a dish a "nasty" name people find it repulsive.

I hope you enjoy the recipes within. Have a happy Halloween!!

KREEPY KATERING

TABLE OF CONTENTS

SPIRITS	1 - 18
UN APPETIZERS	21-40
GHASTLY DISHES	41-56
DEVILISH DESSERTS	57-64

SPIRITS

Every good party should start out with cocktails befitting the occasion. Halloween is no exception to this rule. There are many wines and beer on the market today with Halloween appropriate names. I always serve these at my parties to help set the mood, as well as the cocktails listed here. Black vodka can be found easily at your local store. I find that the wine stores carry theme wines and beers during the season. If you can not find them locally they are available on line.

Rotten Apple Martini
2

Vampire Kiss
4

Mad Scientist
6

Bloody Mary
8

Eyeball Highball
10

Venus Fly Trap
12

Merry Widow
14

Bloody Bubbles
16

Swamp Shots
18

ROTTEN APPLE MARTINI

2 Oz   Black vodka

½ Oz   Sour Apple Mix

½ Oz   Orange Liqueur

¾ Oz   Sour Mix

Combine all ingredients in a cocktail shaker, together with ice cubes. Shake well and strain into a cocktail glass. Garnish with a gummy worm or a slice of dried apple.

VAMPIRE KISS

2 Oz   Peach Snapps

2 Oz   pureed peach

White Wine

Several drops of red food coloring

Place peach snap's and pureed peach into a wine glass. Add food coloring and fill with white wine. Serve in a cocktail glass rimmed with a corn syrup that has been dyed red. Let syrup drip down rim to give the appearance of blood. Fangs can be added to the side of the glass for an even creepier effect.

MAD SCIENTIST

4 ounces   Gin

4 ounces   Sour Mix

A few drops of green food coloring

Pop Rocks

Combine all ingredient in a cocktail shaker, together with ice cubes. Shake well and drain into a cocktail glass. Rim glass with Pop rocks. The rocks will explode when the unknowing guest takes a sip. These can also be served in the large size test tubes.

BLOODY MARY

1 ½ ounces spicy vegetable juice

1 ½ ounces vodka

Worcestershire sauce

Ground black pepper

Hot pepper sauce

Fresh horseradish

Mix ingredients together with ice. Garnish with celery stalk of black olives. The celery can be placed in a glass containing a mixture of food coloring and water several days prior to the party. This will offer a rotting effect without changing the taste.

EYEBALL HIGH BALL

2 ounces bourbon

2 ounces ginger ale

Pour ingredients over eyeball ice cubes.

For ice cubes: Freeze small rubber or gummy eyeballs in ice cube trays.

VENUS FLY TRAP

2 ounces vodka

2 ounces tonic water

Combine ingredients and pour over fly ice cubes

For ice cubes: freeze plastic flies in ice cube trays

MERRY WIDOW

2 ounces black vodka

2 ounces cranberry juice

Place ice in glass. Pour in cranberry juice and then top with the black vodka for a layered effect. Do not mix.

BLOODY BUBBLES

Champagne

Red food coloring

Add a few drops of red food coloring to champagne glass. Add champagne.

SWAMP SHOTS

1 package of green gelatin

1 cup of boiling water

1 cup of vodka

Pour into test tubes and chill in refrigerator. Serve after they are set.

UN - APPETIZERS

Voodoo Stew
22

Pond Slime
24

Maggot Brew
26

Poop On a Cracker
28

Brain Cocktail
30

Moldy Cheese
32

Corpse Bites
34

Snails
36

Crows Liver
38

Eye Of Newt
40

VOODOO STEW

2 tablespoons of olive oil
1 ½ ponds Italian sausage links
2 medium white onions diced
2 medium carrots diced
2 medium celery stalks
3 cans of white beans
1 quart chicken broth
Thyme
parsley
rosemary

In a skillet, sauté vegetables in olive oil over medium-high heat. Then add sausages. Brown but do not cook fully. Remove sausages from pan to cool. In a small bowl mash contents of one can of bean using a fork. Add, broth, sautéed vegetables, and beans to a pot. Sausage should be cool by now. Slice sausage into ¼ inch thick slices and add to contents of the pot. Simmer for 20 - 30 minutes. For added effect chicken feet and chicken hearts can be added.

QUICK FIX: Use you favorite brand of canned white bean soup

POND SLIME

2 ham hocks
3 ½ cups green split peas
12 cups water
2 medium chopped onion
2 medium chopped celery stalks
2 medium chopped carrots
thyme, salt and pepper to taste

Add ham hocks and peas to water. Bring to a boil, then reduce heat and simmer for 2 ½ hours. Add vegetable and seasoning. Continue simmering for another 1 /1/2 hours

QUICK FIX: Use you favorite brand of canned split pea soup

MAGGOT BREW

½ cups of chopped carrot
½ cups of chopped celery
½ cups of chopped onion
¼ cup chopped cilantro
3 cans of black beans
2 cans of spicy tomatoes
1 small can of chopped jalapeño peppers
2 cups of fully cooked orzo pasta (maggots)
salt to taste

Sauté chopped vegetables in a pot. Add vegetables, beans, peppers and tomatoes. Simmer for 20 – 30 minutes. Before serving add cilantro and maggots.

QUICK FIX: Use your favorite brand of canned soup. Add maggots.

POOP ON A CRACKER

1 can of prepared pate
brown food coloring
1 package of water crackers

I like to use canned pate because of the consistency. Stir in a few drops of brown food coloring until the pate resembles "poop". Place the pate in a pastry bag or a Ziploc bag with a hole cut in the corner. Pipe the pate onto the cracker in a circular motion.

BRAIN COCKTAIL

1 skull with open cranium
2 pounds of boiled shrimp
3 cups of red wine vinegar
3 tablespoons of allspice
3 tablespoons of bay leaves

De-vein and chill shrimp. Marinate for up to three days. Place some of the shrimp inside cranium until it reaches top edge. Layer the remaining shrimp into the skull carefully forming the ridges of the brain. A small amount of black food coloring can be added to the marinade to make the shrimp gray.

MOLDY CHEESE

2 - 8 ounce packages of cream cheese
1 cup of crumbled blue cheese
1 ½ teaspoons worchershire sauce
black sesame seeds

Mix together cream cheese, blue cheese and worchershire sauce. Form mixture into a ball. Roll the ball in black sesame seeds. Chill before serving.

QUICK FIX: purchase a pre-prepared cheese ball and roll in black sesame seeds.

I like to serve a fruit and cheese platter with black grapes, black plums, figs and a sliced open pomegranate. This makes for a ghastly display.

CORPSE BITES

1 package of smoked herring
1 package of pumpernickel bread
Horseradish

Using a small cookie cutter, cut bread into bite size rounds. Add a small slice of smoked fish and top with a dollop of horseradish.

SNAILS

(Just Gross Enough)

3 packages of hors d'oever shells
6 dozen canned escargot
1 stick of butter
chopped garlic and parsley to taste

In a sauté pan melt butter. Place escargot and herbs into melted butter. When the butter begins to boil, remove pan from heat. While the snails are cooking, preheat shells in a warm oven . Add one snail per shell. Adding too much liquid will make the shells soggy.

CROWS LIVER

1 tin of smoked oysters

1 box of multi grain crackers

Place a smoked oyster on each cracker and serve.

EYE OF NEWT

1 box of pancake mix
Crème Fraiche
Caviar

Prepare pancake mix according to directions. Cook in 2 inch circles. Top with crème fraiche and caviar.

GHASTLY DISHES

GHASTLY DISHES

Slimy Bat Wings
44

Bloody Ribs
46

Earthworm Pie
48

Grave Yard Mold
50

Flies and Maggots
52

Vampire Entrails
54

Night Crawlers
56

SLIMY BAT WINGS

5 Pounds of chicken wings (leave tips on)
2 ½ cups of dark soy sauce
2 cups of brown sugar
1 cup of honey
Black paste food coloring
Salt and pepper to taste

Parboil the wings. Drain and place in a deep roasting pan. While the wings are boiling prepare the sauce. Place all remaining ingredients into a pot and boil until sugar melts. Stir constantly with a whisk. Pour mixture over the wings coating evenly. Bake in a 350 degree oven for 20 minutes. Remove the wings from the roasting pan and place on a broiler. Broil for 10 minutes. This will bake the sauce into the wings.

BLOODY RIBS

4 pounds of beef ribs
2 large jars of sweet and sour sauce
red food coloring

Cut up ribs before cooking. Place in a 350 degree oven for 35 to 40 minutes. Add red food coloring to sweet and sour sauce. Drain the ribs and coat well with sauce. Place in the oven for 10 more minutes. Serve hot.

EARTHWORM PIE

1 package of puff pastry shells
2 pounds of beef stew
1 cup chopped onion
2 cans beefy mushroom soup

Brown beef and onion in a saucepan. Add cans of beefy mushroom soup and simmer for 45 minutest or until tender. While the beef is simmering. Cook pastry shells in a 400 degree oven for 20 – 25 minutes. Fill and serve. Garnish with an earthworm.

GRAVE YARD MOLD

3 cups of cooked rice (maggots)
1 cup of minced onion
1 large bag of frozen spinach
1 cup of cottage cheese
½ cup of feta cheese
2 eggs

Preheat the oven to 375 degrees. In a skillet sauté onions until soft. Add the spinach . Drain. In a large bowl combine all remaining ingredients. Fold in spinach. Spray a casserole dish with cooking spray. Pour mixture into casserole and bake for 20-25 minutes.

FLIES AND MAGGOTS

3 cans of black beans
5 cups of water
6 cups of cooked rice
2 cups of chopped onion
1 garlic clove chopped
salt to taste

In a large pot stir together all ingredients. Simmer until water cooks down. Remove 1/3 of the beans and mash. Return the beans to the pot.

Serve in a bowl and garnish with plastic flies.

QUICK FIX: Use a package of black beans and rice mix

VAMPIRE ENTRAILS

1 large package of fettuccini pasta
1 jar of prepared Alfredo sauce
red food coloring

Boil pasta for 7-9 minutes and drain. Heat Alfredo sauce adding a few drops of food coloring until is bright red. Pour sauce over pasta. Mix and serve.

NIGHT CRAWLERS

1 package of black squid ink pasta
2 cups of mixed mushrooms
1 clove of minced garlic
3 table spoons of olive oil

Boil pasta for 7-9 minutes. Drain. Sauté mushrooms in oil and garlic. Mix together with pasta and serve.

Black squid ink pasta can be found in specialty stores

DEVILISH DESSERTS

DEVILISH DESSERTS

Kitty Litter Cake
60

Shrunken Head
62

Bloody Butcher Cake
64

KITTY LITTER CAKE

1 box of spice cake mix
1 box of white cake mix
2 large boxes of pudding
1 bag of small tootsie rolls
1 box of vanilla wafer cookies
green food coloring
1 new kitty litter pan
1 new pooper scooper

Bake cake mixes according to directions. Prepare pudding according to direction. Crumble cakes into kitty litter pan. Mix in enough pudding to moisten.

Crumb wafer cookies in a food processor. Add a few drops of green food coloring. Mix until it has the appearance of litter.

Sprinkle "litter" over the top of the cake.

Microwave one tootsie roll at a time for a few seconds. Just warn them. Taper the ends of give it a fresh poop effect. Scatter them through out the litter box. Place one over the side.

Serve cake with the pooper scooper.

SHRUNKEN HEADS

1 dozen cored apples.
2 cups of brown sugar
Cinnamon

Carve a face into the apple. Fill center of apple with the brown sugar and sprinkle with cinnamon. Bake in a 350 degree oven for 45 minutes.

BLOODY BUTCHER CAKE

1 box of white cake mix
5 large eggs
½ cup of vegetable oil
1 cup of buttermilk
2 bottles of red food coloring (2 ounces each)
2 cans of whipped cream cheese icing
1 fake bloody hand

Add mix to bowl. Mix in eggs one at a time. Add oil and buttermilk. Mix thoroughly then add the two bottles of red food coloring. Pour batter into greased and floured layer pans. Bake according to package directions.

Ice with whipped cream cheese icing.

Place hand upright in the center of the cake

www.ingramcontent.com/pod-product-compliance
Lightning Source LLC
Chambersburg PA
CBHW041552220426
43666CB00002B/40